Piano • VOCAL • GUITAR

Still More SONGS OF THE NINETIES

THE DECADE SERIES

ISBN 0-634-01565-6

HAL•LEONARD®
CORPORATION

7777 W. BLUEMOUND RD. P.O. BOX 13819 MILWAUKEE, WI 53213

Visit Hal Leonard Online at
www.halleonard.com

CONTENTS

ADIA

Words and Music by SARAH McLACHLAN
and PIERRE MARCHAND

A - di - a, I do ___ be - lieve ___ I failed ___ you. ___

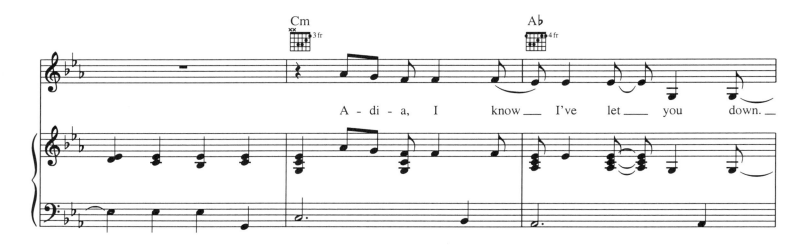

A - di - a, I know ___ I've let ___ you down. ___

Don't you know I tried ___ so hard ___ to

AND SO IT GOES

Words and Music by
BILLY JOEL

Slow Ballad, with much rubato

ANGEL

Words and Music by
SARAH McLACHLAN

Original key: Db major. This edition has been transposed down one half-step to be more playable.

THEME FROM ANGELA'S ASHES

Paramount Pictures and Universal Pictures International present ANGELA'S ASHES

Music by
JOHN WILLIAMS

Gently flowing

As If We Never Said Goodbye

from SUNSET BOULEVARD

Music by ANDREW LLOYD WEBBER
Lyrics by DON BLACK and CHRISTOPHER HAMPTON,
with contributions by AMY POWERS

BARELY BREATHING

Words and Music by
DUNCAN SHEIK

FIELDS OF GOLD

Written and Composed by
STING

44

FROM A DISTANCE

Words and Music by
JULIE GOLD

FOR THE FIRST TIME

Words and Music by ALLAN RICH,
JAMES NEWTON HOWARD and JUD FRIEDMAN

FREE AS A BIRD

Beatles version by JOHN LENNON, PAUL McCARTNEY,
GEORGE HARRISON and RINGO STARR

THE GIFT

Words and Music by TOM DOUGLAS
and JIM BRICKMAN

Slow Ballad

Female: Hoo.

Win-ter snow is fall-ing down, chil-dren laugh-ing all a-round,

lights are turn-ing on, like a fair-y tale come true.

THE HARDEST THING

Words and Music by STEVE KIPNER
and DAVID FRANK

GOD HELP THE OUTCASTS

from Walt Disney's THE HUNCHBACK OF NOTRE DAME

Music by ALAN MENKEN
Lyrics by STEPHEN SCHWARTZ

Lyrics:
I don't know if You can hear me or if You're e-ven there. I don't know if You will

lis - ten to a hum - ble prayer. They tell me I am just an

out - cast; I should - n't speak to You. Still I see Your face and

won - der: were You once an out - cast, too? _____

God help the out - casts
I ask for noth - ing,

HOLD MY HAND

Words and Music by DARIUS CARLOS RUCKER, EVERETT DEAN FELBER,
MARK WILLIAM BRYAN and JAMES GEORGE SONEFELD

I DRIVE MYSELF CRAZY

Words and Music by RICK NOWELS,
ELLEN SHIPLEY and ALAN RICH

Moderately slow

HYMN TO THE FALLEN

from the Paramount and DreamWorks Motion Picture SAVING PRIVATE RYAN

Music by
JOHN WILLIAMS

Slowly, reverently

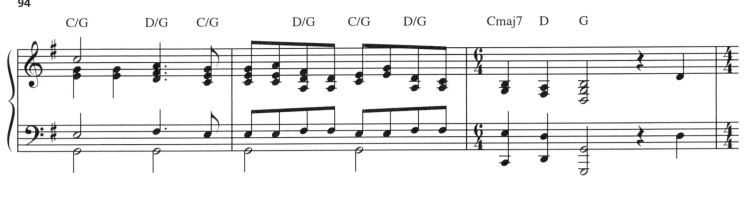

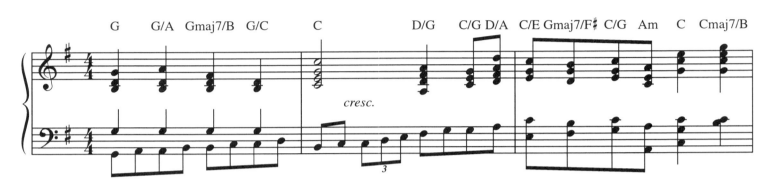

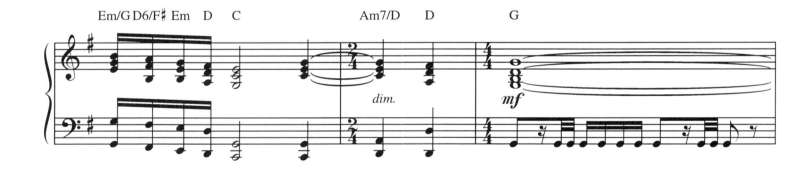

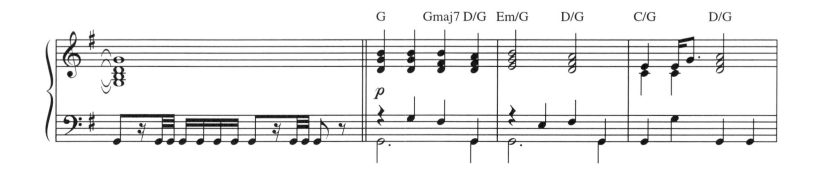

Broadly and expansively

I BELIEVE IN YOU AND ME

from the Touchstone Motion Picture THE PREACHER'S WIFE

Words and Music by DAVID WOLFERT
and SANDY LINZER

I WANT TO SPEND MY LIFETIME LOVING YOU

from the TriStar Motion Picture THE MASK OF ZORRO

Music by JAMES HORNER
Lyric by WILL JENNINGS

Male: Moon so bright, night so fine, keep your heart here with mine.

Life's a dream _____ we are dream - ing. _____

Female: Race the moon, __ catch the wind, __ ride the night

he - roes fall. _ Rise a - gain, win it all. _____

Female: In your heart, _ can't you feel the glo - ry? _____

Through our joy, through our pain, _ *Both:* we can move worlds a - gain. ___

Take my hand, _____ dance _ with me. *Male:* Dance _ with me. *Both:* I want to

I WILL REMEMBER YOU

Theme from THE BROTHERS McMULLEN

Words and Music by SARAH McLACHLAN,
SEAMUS EGAN and DAVE MERENDA

I WILL BE HERE

Words and Music by
STEVEN CURTIS CHAPMAN

I'LL BE

Words and Music by
EDWIN McCAIN

Original key: B major. This edition has been transposed up one half-step to be more playable.

123

IF I EVER LOSE MY FAITH IN YOU

Written and Composed by
STING

132

IRIS
from the Motion Picture CITY OF ANGELS

Words and Music by
JOHN RZEZNIK

And I _____ don't want the world _____ to see _____ me

JUMP, JIVE AN' WAIL

Words and Music by
LOUIS PRIMA

KISS ME

as featured in the Miramax Motion Picture SHE'S ALL THAT

Words and Music by
MATT SLOCUM

Moderate beat (♩ = 96)

Kiss ___ me out of the beard - ed bar-ley, ___
Kiss ___ me down by the bro - ken tree-house, ___

___ night - ly, be - side the green, ___ green grass. ___
___ swing ___ me up - on its hang - ing tire. ___

MAMBO NO. 5
(A Little Bit Of...)

Original Music by DAMASO PEREZ PRADO
Words by LOU BEGA and ZIPPY

Relaxed two-beat feel

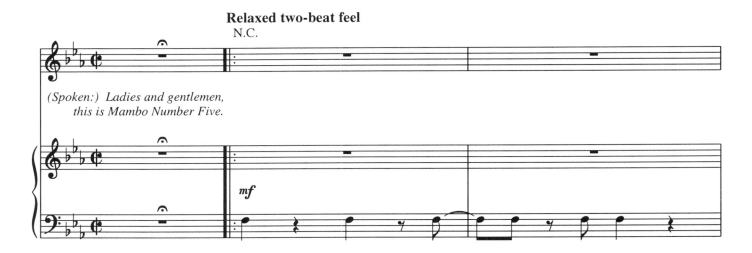

(Spoken:) Ladies and gentlemen,
this is Mambo Number Five.

One, two, _ three, four, five. _ Ev-'ry-

bod-y in the car. So, come on, let's ride _ to the li-quor store a-round the

REAL LOVE

Words and Music by
JOHN LENNON

All my lit-tle plans and schemes, __ lost like some for-got-ten dreams.

Seems that all I real-ly was doin' ___ was wait-in' for

REFLECTION
from Walt Disney Pictures' MULAN

Music by MATTHEW WILDER
Lyrics by DAVID ZIPPEL

Moderately slow

Look at me, you may think you see who I really am, but you'll never know me. Ev-'ry day it's as if I play a part.

SEASONS OF LOVE

from RENT

Words and Music by
JONATHAN LARSON

SOMEONE LIKE YOU

from JEKYLL & HYDE

Words by LESLIE BRICUSSE
Music by FRANK WILDHORN

Slowly, with expression

I peered through win-dows, watched life go by. Dreamed of to-mor-row,
It's like you took my dreams, made each one real. You reached in-side of me

but stayed in-side. The past was hold-ing me,
and made me feel. And now I see a world

SOMETHING TO TALK ABOUT
(Let's Give Them Something to Talk About)
from SOMETHING TO TALK ABOUT

Words and Music by
SHIRLEY EIKHARD

Moderate Reggae/Rock

Peo - ple are talk - ing, talk - ing a - bout peo - ple.___
I feel so fool - ish. I nev - er no - ticed that,___

I hear them whis - per, you won't___ be - lieve it.
ba - by, you're act - ing so nerv - ous, like___ you're fall - ing.

* Recorded a half step lower

Give a lit-tle some-thing to talk a - bout,_____ babe.__ I got some mys-t'ry, why don't

you just fig-ure out._____ Give them some-thing to talk a - bout. How a - bout

love?_____ Wooh,____

lis-ten up, ba-by. A lit-tle mys-t'ry won't hurt.—

Give them some-thing to talk a-bout. How a-bout— love?—

THIS IS THE MOMENT
from JEKYLL & HYDE

Words by LESLIE BRICUSSE
Music by FRANK WILDHORN

This is the

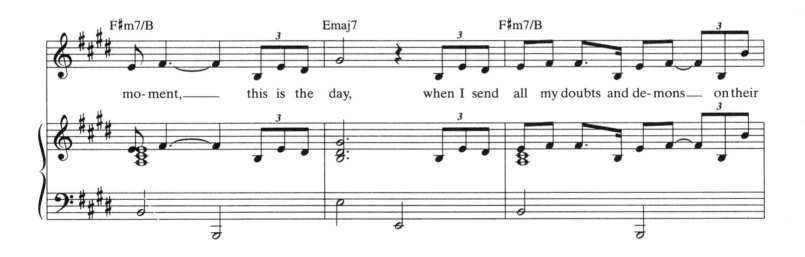

mo-ment,___ this is the day, when I send all my doubts and de-mons___ on their

way. Ev-'ry en-deav-our___ I have made ev-er___ is

com-ing____ in-to play, is here and now____ to-day.____ This is the

mo-ment,____ this is the time when the mo-men-tum and the mo-ment are in

rhyme. Give me this mo-ment,____ this____ pre-cious chance. I'll

gath-er____ up my past and make some sense_ at last. This is the

TO LOVE YOU MORE

Words and Music by DAVID FOSTER
and JUNIOR MILES

WHEN YOU BELIEVE
(From The Prince of Egypt)

Words and Music Composed by STEPHEN SCHWARTZ
with Additional Music by BABYFACE

TORN

Words and Music by PHIL THORNALLEY,
SCOTT CUTLER and ANNE PREVIN

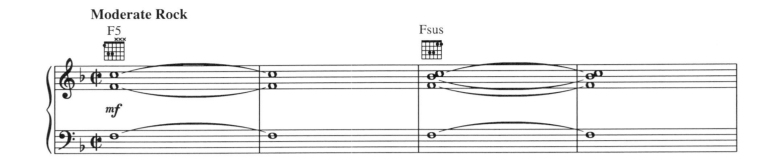

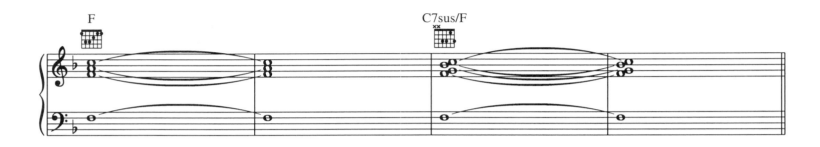

Torn. _____

Guitar solo - ad lib.

Repeat and Fade | **Optional Ending**

WHISTLE DOWN THE WIND
from WHISTLE DOWN THE WIND

Music by ANDREW LLOYD WEBBER
Lyrics by JIM STEINMAN

Swallow & Boone

I'll be there to hold you I'll be there to stop the chills and all the weep - ing——— Make it

clear and strong——— so the whole night long——— Ev - ery

sig - nal that you send un - til the ve - ry end I will not a - ban - don you my prec-ious friend So

try and stem the tide——— Then you'll raise a ban - ner——— Send a

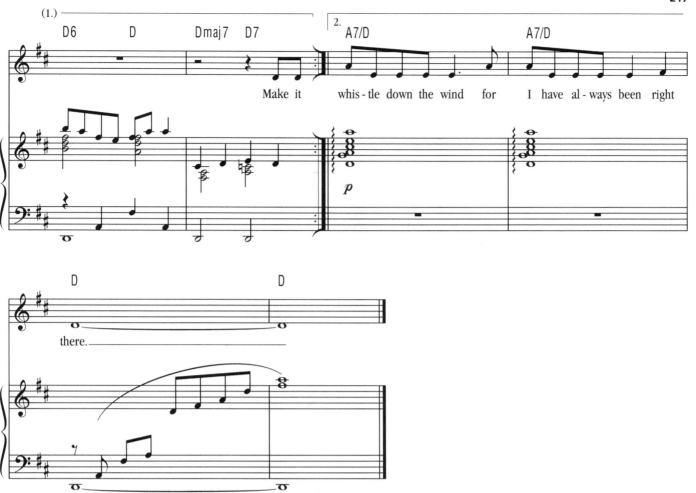

(1.)

D6   D   Dmaj7   D7 | 2. A7/D   A7/D

Make it   whis-tle down the wind   for   I have al-ways been right

D   D

there.

WRITTEN IN THE STARS

from Walt Disney Theatrical Productions' AIDA

Music by ELTON JOHN
Lyrics by TIM RICE

YOU'LL BE IN MY HEART

(Pop Version)

from Walt Disney Pictures' TARZAN™

Words and Music by
PHIL COLLINS

YOU'VE GOT A FRIEND IN ME

from Walt Disney's TOY STORY
from Walt Disney Pictures' TOY STORY 2 - A Pixar Film

Music and Lyrics by
RANDY NEWMAN

You've got a friend in me.
You've got a friend in me.

You've got a friend in me.
You've got a friend in me.

When the road looks rough a-head and you're miles
You got trou-bles, then I got 'em too.

ZOOT SUIT RIOT

Words and Music by
STEVE PERRY

Original key: A♭ minor. This edition has been transposed up one half-step to be more playable.

THE DECADE SERIES

The Decade Series explores the music of the 1890s to the 1980s through each era's major events and personalities. Each volume features text and photos and over 40 of the decade's top songs, showing how music has acted as a mirror or a catalyst for current events and trends. All books are arranged for piano, voice and guitar.

Songs Of The 1890's

55 songs, including: Asleep In The Deep • Hello! Ma Baby • Maple Leaf Rag • My Wild Irish Rose • 'O Sole Mio • The Sidewalks Of New York • Stars And Stripes Forever • Ta Ra Ra Boom De Ay • When You Were Sweet Sixteen • and more.
00311655 ....$12.95

Songs Of The 1900's – 1900-1909

57 favorites, including: By The Light Of The Silvery Moon • Fascination • Give My Regards To Broadway • Glow Worm • Meet Me In St. Louis • Take Me Out To The Ball Game • Yankee Doodle Boy • and more.
00311656 ....$12.95

Songs Of The 1910's

57 classics, including: After You've Gone • Ah! Sweet Mystery Of Life • Danny Boy • Let Me Call You Sweetheart • My Melancholy Baby • Oh, You Beautiful Doll • When Irish Eyes Are Smiling • You Made Me Love You (I Didn't Want To Do It) • and more.
00311657 ....$12.95

Songs Of The 20's

58 songs, featuring: Ain't Misbehavin' • April Showers • Baby Face • California Here I Come • Five Foot Two, Eyes Of Blue • I Can't Give You Anything But Love • Manhattan • Stardust • The Varsity Drag • Who's Sorry Now.
00361122 ....$14.95

Songs Of The 30's

61 songs, featuring: All Of Me • The Continental • I Can't Get Started • I'm Getting Sentimental Over You • In The Mood • The Lady Is A Tramp • Love Letters In The Sand • My Funny Valentine • Smoke Gets In Your Eyes • What A Diff'rence A Day Made.
00361123 ....$14.95

Songs Of The 40's

61 songs, featuring: God Bless The Child • How High The Moon • The Last Time I Saw Paris • Moonlight In Vermont • A Nightingale Sang In Berkeley Square • A String Of Pearls • Swinging On A Star • Tuxedo Junction • You'll Never Walk Alone.
00361124 ....$14.95

Songs Of The 50's

59 songs, featuring: Blue Suede Shoes • Blue Velvet • Here's That Rainy Day • Love Me Tender • Misty • Rock Around The Clock • Satin Doll • Tammy • Three Coins In The Fountain • Young At Heart.
00361125 ....$14.95

Songs Of The 60's

60 songs, featuring: By The Time I Get To Phoenix • California Dreamin' • Can't Help Falling In Love • Downtown • Green Green Grass Of Home • Happy Together • I Want To Hold Your Hand • Love Is Blue • More • Strangers In The Night.
00361126 ....$14.95

Songs Of The 70's

More than 45 songs including: Don't Cry For Me Argentina • Feelings • The First Time Ever I Saw Your Face • How Deep Is Your Love • Imagine • Let It Be • Me And Bobby McGee • Piano Man • Send In The Clowns • You Don't Bring Me Flowers • You Needed Me.
00361127 ....$14.95

Songs Of The 80's

Over 40 of this decade's biggest hits, including: Candle In The Wind • Don't Worry, Be Happy • Ebony And Ivory • Endless Love • Every Breath You Take • Flashdance...What A Feeling • Islands In The Stream • Kokomo • Memory • Sailing • Somewhere Out There • We Built This City • What's Love Got To Do With It • With Or Without You.
00490275 ....$14.95

Due to popular demand, we are pleased to present these new collections with even more great songs from the 1920s through 1980s. Each book features beautiful piano/vocal/guitar arrangements. Perfect for practicing musicians, educators, collectors, and music hobbyists.

More Songs Of The 20's

Over 50 songs, including: Ain't We Got Fun? • Bill • Carolina In The Morning • Fascinating Rhythm • The Hawaiian Wedding Song • Malagueña • Nobody Knows You When You're Down And Out • Someone To Watch Over Me • Yes, Sir, That's My Baby • and more.
00311647 ....$14.95

More Songs of the 30's

Over 50 songs, including: All The Things You Are • A Fine Romance • In A Sentimental Mood • Just A Gigolo • Let's Call The Whole Thing Off • Mad Dogs And Englishmen • Stompin' At The Savoy • Stormy Weather • Thanks For The Memory • and more.
00311648 ....$14.95

More Songs Of The 40's

Over 60 songs, including: Bali Ha'i • Be Careful, It's My Heart • Five Guys Named Moe • The Last Time I Saw Paris • Old Devil Moon • San Antonio Rose • Some Enchanted Evening • Too Darn Hot • and more.
00311649 ....$14.95

More Songs Of The 50's

56 songs, including: Blueberry Hill • Chanson D'Amour • Charlie Brown • Do-Re-Mi • Hey, Good Lookin' • Hound Dog • I Could Have Danced All Night • Mack The Knife • Mona Lisa • My Favorite Things • (Let Me Be Your) Teddy Bear • That's Amore • and more.
00311650 ....$14.95

FOR MORE INFORMATION, SEE YOUR LOCAL MUSIC DEALER, OR WRITE TO:

HAL•LEONARD®
CORPORATION
7777 W. BLUEMOUND RD. P.O. BOX 13819 MILWAUKEE, WI 53213

Prices, contents, and availability subject to change without notice
Some products may not be available outside the U.S.A.

More Songs Of The 60's

66 songs, including: Alfie • Baby Elephant Walk • Bonanza • Born To Be Wild • Eleanor Rigby • Moon River • Raindrops Keep Fallin' On My Head • Seasons In The Sun • Sweet Caroline • Tell Laura I Love Her • What The World Needs Now • Wooly Bully • and more.
00311651 ....$14.95

More Songs Of The 70's

Over 50 songs, including: Afternoon Delight • All By Myself • American Pie • Billy, Don't Be A Hero • Happy Days • Honesty • I Shot The Sheriff • Maggie May • Maybe I'm Amazed • She Believes In Me • She's Always A Woman • Wishing You Were Here • and more.
00311652 ....$14.95

More Songs Of The 80's

43 songs, including: Addicted To Love • Call Me • Don't Know Much • Footloose • Girls Just Want To Have Fun • The Heat Is On • Karma Chameleon • Longer • Straight Up • Take My Breath Away • Tell Her About It • We're In This Love Together • and more.
00311653 ....$14.95

What could be better than even *more* songs from your favorite decade! These books feature piano/vocal/guitar arrangements with no duplication with *earlier volumes*.

Still More Songs Of The 30's

Over 50 songs including: April in Paris • Body And Soul • Heat Wave • It Don't Mean A Thing (If It Ain't Got That Swing) • and more.
00310027 ....$14.95

Still More Songs Of The 40's

Over 50 songs including: Any Place I Hang My Hat • Don't Get Around Much Anymore • If I Loved You • Sentimental Journey • and more.
00310028 ....$14.95

Still More Songs Of The 50's

Over 50 songs including: Autumn Leaves • Chantilly Lace • If I Were A Bell • Luck Be A Lady • The Man That Got Away • Venus • and more.
00310029 ....$14.95

Still More Songs Of The 60's

Over 50 more songs, including: Do You Know The Way To San Jose • Duke Of Earl • Hey Jude • I'm Henry VIII, I Am • Leader Of The Pack • (You Make Me Feel) Like A Natural Woman • What A Wonderful World • and more.
00311680 ....$14.95

Still More Songs Of The 70's

Over 60 hits, including: Cat's In The Cradle • Nadia's Theme • Philadelphia Freedom • The Way We Were • You've Got A Friend • and more.
00311683 ....$14.95

Contemporary Classics

Your favorite songs for piano, voice and guitar.

The Definitive Rock 'n' Roll Collection
A classic collection of the best songs from the early rock 'n' roll years – 1955-1966. 97 songs, including: Barbara Ann • Chantilly Lace • Dream Lover • Duke of Earl • Earth Angel • Great Balls of Fire • Louie, Louie • Rock Around the Clock • Ruby Baby • Runaway • (Seven Little Girls) Sitting in the Back Seat • Stay • Surfin' U.S.A. • Wild Thing • Woolly Bully • and more.
00490195 ....$27.95

The Big Book of Rock
78 of rock's biggest hits, including: Addicted to Love • American Pie • Born to Be Wild • Cold As Ice • Dust in the Wind • Free Bird • Goodbye Yellow Brick Road • Groovin' • Hey Jude • I Love Rock 'N' Roll • Lay Down Sally • Layla • Livin' on a Prayer • Louie Louie • Maggie May • Me and Bobby McGee • Monday, Monday • Owner of a Lonely Heart • Shout • Walk This Way • We Didn't Start the Fire • You Really Got Me • and more.
00311566...$19.95

Big Book of Movie Music
Features 73 classic songs from 72 movies: Beauty and the Beast • Change the World • Eye of the Tiger • I Finally Found Someone • The John Dunbar Theme • Somewhere in Time • Stayin' Alive • Take My Breath Away • Unchained Melody • The Way You Look Tonight • You've Got a Friend in Me • Zorro's Theme • more.
00311582 ....$19.95

The Best Rock Songs Ever
70 of the best rock songs from yesterday and today, including: All Day and All of the Night • All Shook Up • Ballroom Blitz • Bennie and the Jets • Blue Suede Shoes • Born to Be Wild • Boys Are Back in Town • Every Breath You Take • Free Bird • Hey Jude • I Still Haven't Found What I'm Looking For • Livin' on a Prayer • Lola • Louie Louie • Maggie May • Money • (She's) Some Kind of Wonderful • Takin' Care of Business • Walk This Way • We Didn't Start the Fire • We Got the Beat • Wild Thing • more!
00490424 ....$17.95

#1 Songs of the '90s
21 top hits as listed on the *Billboard* Hot 100 Singles Chart. Songs include: All My Life • Candle in the Wind 1997 • The Power of Love • The Sign • and more.
00310018...$12.95

Motown Anthology
This songbook commemorates Motown's 40th Anniversary with 68 songs, background information on this famous record label, and lots of photos. Songs include: ABC • Baby Love • Ben • Dancing in the Street • Easy • For Once in My Life • My Girl • Shop Around • The Tracks of My Tears • War • What's Going On • You Can't Hurry Love • and many more.
00310367 ....$19.95

"My Heart Will Go On (Love Theme from 'Titanic')" & 23 More Songs from Today's Hit Movies
Includes these megahits: (I Love You) For Sentimental Reasons (*As Good As It Gets*) • You Must Love Me (*Evita*) • Miss Misery (*Good Will Hunting*) • You Sexy Thing (*The Full Monty*) • I Say a Little Prayer (*My Best Friend's Wedding*) • and more.
00310417...$10.95

Women of Modern Rock
25 songs from contemporary chanteuses, including: As I Lay Me Down • Connection • Feed the Tree • Galileo • Here and Now • Look What Love Has Done • Love Sneakin' Up on You • Walking on Broken Glass • You Oughta Know • Zombie • and more.
00310093 ....$14.95

Jock Rock Hits
32 stadium-shaking favorites, including: Another One Bites the Dust • The Boys Are Back in Town • Freeze-Frame • Gonna Make You Sweat (Everybody Dance Now) • I Got You (I Feel Good) • Na Na Hey Hey Kiss Him Goodbye • Rock & Roll – Part II (The Hey Song) • Shout • Tequila • We Are the Champions • We Will Rock You • Whoomp! (There It Is) • Wild Thing • and more.
00310105 ....$14.95

Rock Ballads
31 sentimental favorites, including: All for Love • Bed of Roses • Dust in the Wind • Everybody Hurts • Right Here Waiting • Tears in Heaven • and more.
00311673..$14.95

FOR MORE INFORMATION, SEE YOUR LOCAL MUSIC DEALER,
OR WRITE TO:

HAL•LEONARD™ CORPORATION
7777 W. BLUEMOUND RD. P.O. BOX 13819 MILWAUKEE, WI 53213

Visit Hal Leonard Online at www.halleonard.com

Prices, contents & availability subject to change without notice.

0300